My Scripture Workbook

BIBLE VERSES ABOUT

Living as a New Creation

this book belongs to:

_____

Dear Parents,

Thank you for choosing this resource! All Scripture is breathed out by God and is the source of divine, absolute authority (2 Timothy 3:16-17). His Word is necessary for us to be complete and equipped for every good work He has prepared in advance for us to do. It is sufficient for all of our needs—it comforts, convicts, and nourishes us to grow in godliness (John 17:17). It is also the weapon by which we can overcome the desires of our flesh and the assaults of the enemy (Ephesians 6:17).

Therefore, teaching the Word to our children is a worthy investment of our time and energy. We are responsible for guarding our children's minds, and we should endeavor to fill them with God's Word. This can be done in many ways—engagement in a local church, intentional conversations, direct recitation of verses, an audio Bible, family devotionals, and transcription.

Transcription is a championed practice for children for many reasons. It improves penmanship, advances spelling skills, and presents proper sentence structures. But more importantly, it is a powerful aid in memorization. It encourages children to slow down and employ many of their senses to engage the text at hand. It also provides the opportunity to dig deeper into a memory verse by providing the time and space for discussion between the parent and the child.

My Scripture Workbook is a tool for parents to help their children hide God's Word in their hearts. Parents are given more focused time with the child to discuss the passage. As a child transcribes the verse on the dotted lines, they learn to store Scripture in his or her mind. This is one tool to equip our children with memorization strategies, which are skills that will last a lifetime and greatly enhance their ability to hide God's Word in their minds and hearts.

Helpful Tips

- The workbook can be completed at any pace, but a mastery approach is recommended.

- The child can begin their journey of memorization by reading the verse aloud and then transcribing it in the workbook. They can then read it aloud a few more times.

- The following day, the parent and child can approach the same verse in a different way. Some options could be creating hand motions or drawing a picture to represent the verse. Perhaps they can create a rhythm by clapping their hands as they read the verse, allowing the simple cadence to cement the verse in their minds.

- The workbook provides ease for reviewing prior verses. Mastered memory work often requires periodic review.

- The truths listed at the top of each page can be the basis for training children on who they are in Christ and how they can live as a new creation in Christ. While all children need to develop a faith of their own, this workbook provides a common working ground for the parent and child.

- It is important to note that if a memory verse is part of a bigger sentence, we do not end the verse with a period. Rather, we end it with the punctuation used in the Bible. Talk this over with your child, as we know some children are beginning to learn punctuation.

Table of Contents by Reference

Psalm 139:17-18	80	2 Corinthians 5:20	68
Proverbs 10:28	84	Galatians 2:20	8
Matthew 5:14	72	Galatians 5:1	12
John 1:12	32	Galatians 5:14	96
John 8:36	16	Galatians 5:16	82
John 14:15-16	102	Galatians 5:25-26	98
John 15:4	44	Ephesians 2:4-5	78
John 15:10	46	Ephesians 5:8	74
John 15:16	48	Ephesians 5:11	18
Romans 5:1	76	Philippians 3:20	64
Romans 6:1-2	26	Philippians 4:12	90
Romans 6:6	36	Philippians 4:19	70
Romans 6:8	24	Colossians 2:6-7	66
Romans 6:11	10	Colossians 3:1	14
Romans 6:14	22	Colossians 3:9-10	50
Romans 8:1	6	Colossians 3:13	52
Romans 8:37	42	Colossians 3:14-15	54
Romans 12:2	30	Colossians 3:16	56
Romans 15:13	88	Colossians 3:17	58
1 Corinthians 6:17	34	Colossians 3:20	60
1 Corinthians 6:20	20	Colossians 3:23	62
1 Corinthians 12:27	38	1 Peter 1:8-9	86
1 Corinthians 15:58	100	1 Peter 2:9	40
2 Corinthians 5:15	92	1 John 1:7	94
2 Corinthians 5:17	4	1 John 1:9	28

You are a new creation.

Copy today's Bible verse on the next page.

Therefore, if anyone is in Christ, he is a new creation; the old has passed away, and see, the new has come!

2 Corinthians 5:17

First, write your name.

Then, write the verse.

There is no condemnation in Christ.

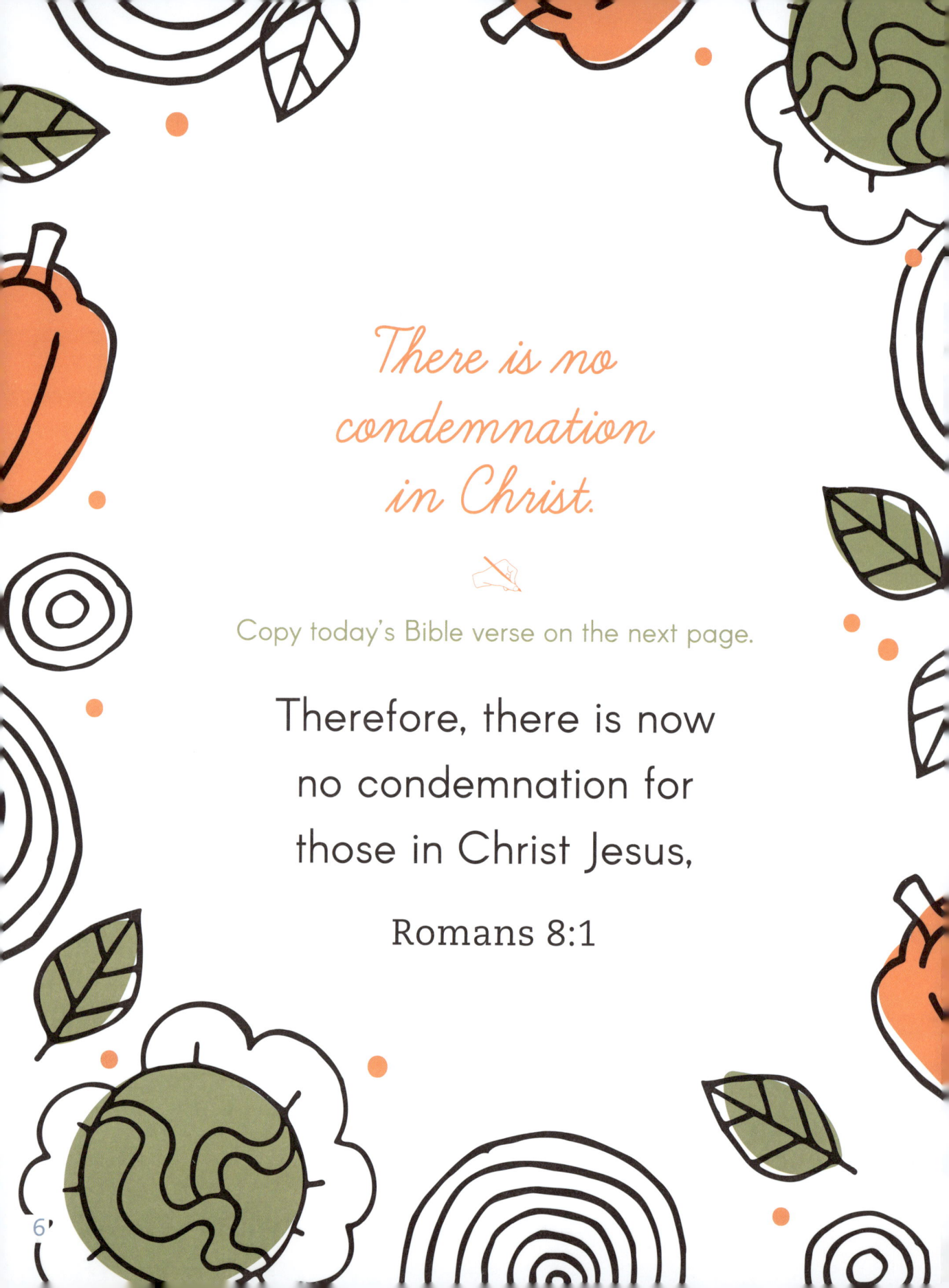

Copy today's Bible verse on the next page.

Therefore, there is now no condemnation for those in Christ Jesus,

Romans 8:1

First, write your name.

Then, write the verse.

Christ lives in you.

Copy today's Bible verse on the next page.

I have been crucified with Christ, and I no longer live, but Christ lives in me. The life I now live in the body, I live by faith in the Son of God, who loved me and gave himself for me.

Galatians 2:20

First, write
your name.

Then, write
the verse.

You are alive in Christ.

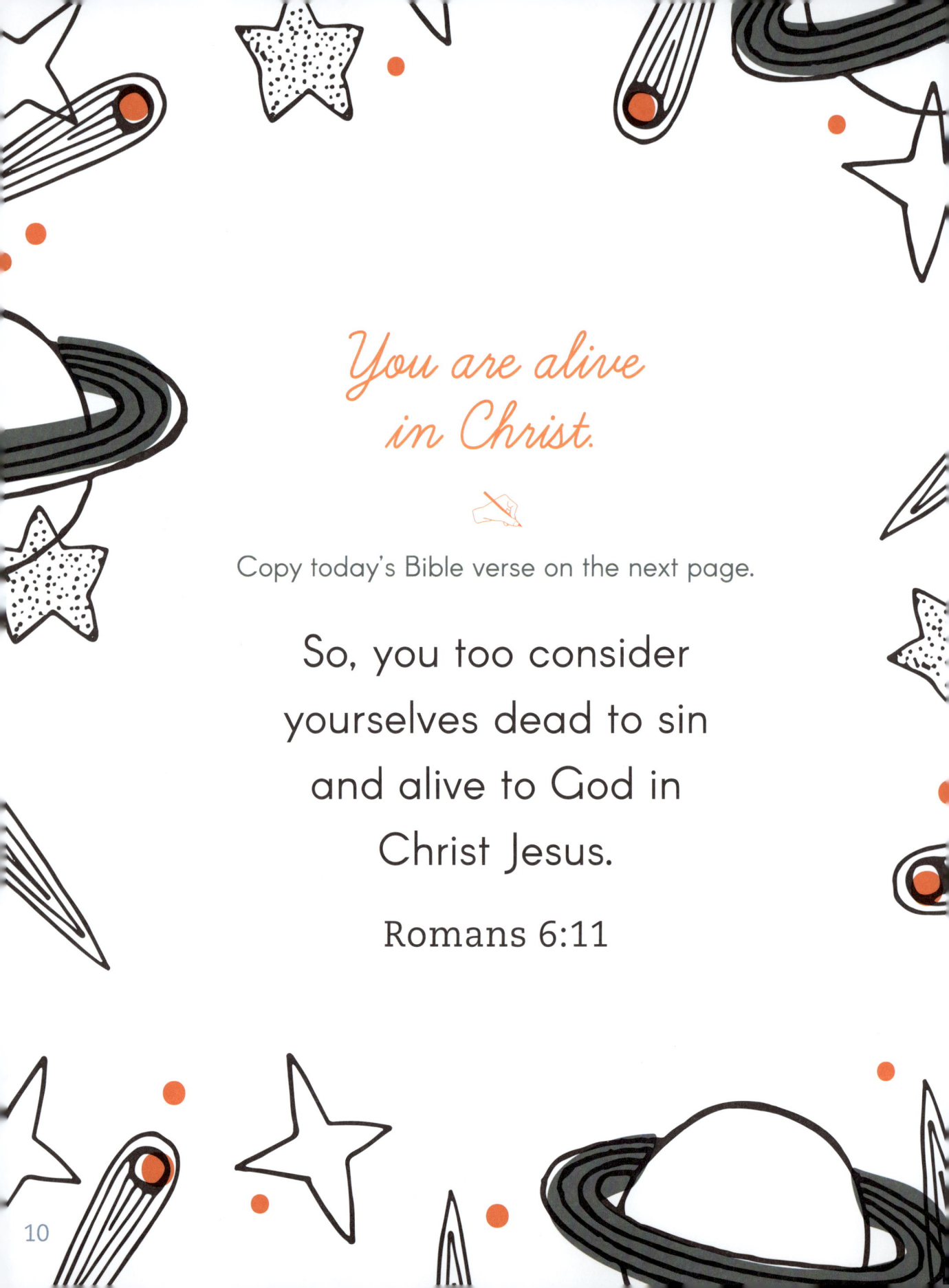

Copy today's Bible verse on the next page.

So, you too consider yourselves dead to sin and alive to God in Christ Jesus.

Romans 6:11

First, write your name.

Then, write the verse.

Christ set you free.

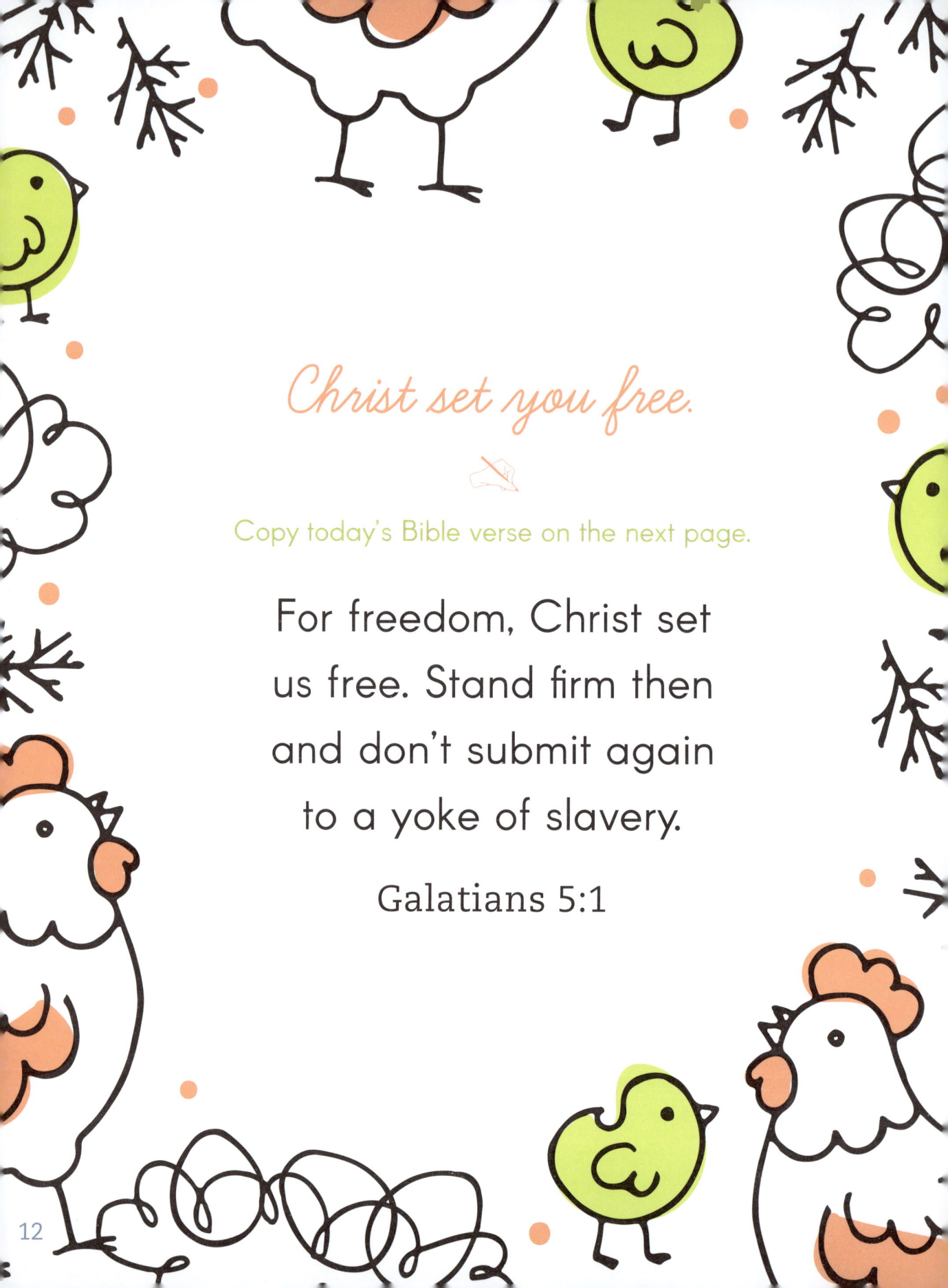

Copy today's Bible verse on the next page.

For freedom, Christ set us free. Stand firm then and don't submit again to a yoke of slavery.

Galatians 5:1

First, write your name.

Then, write the verse.

Seek Christ.

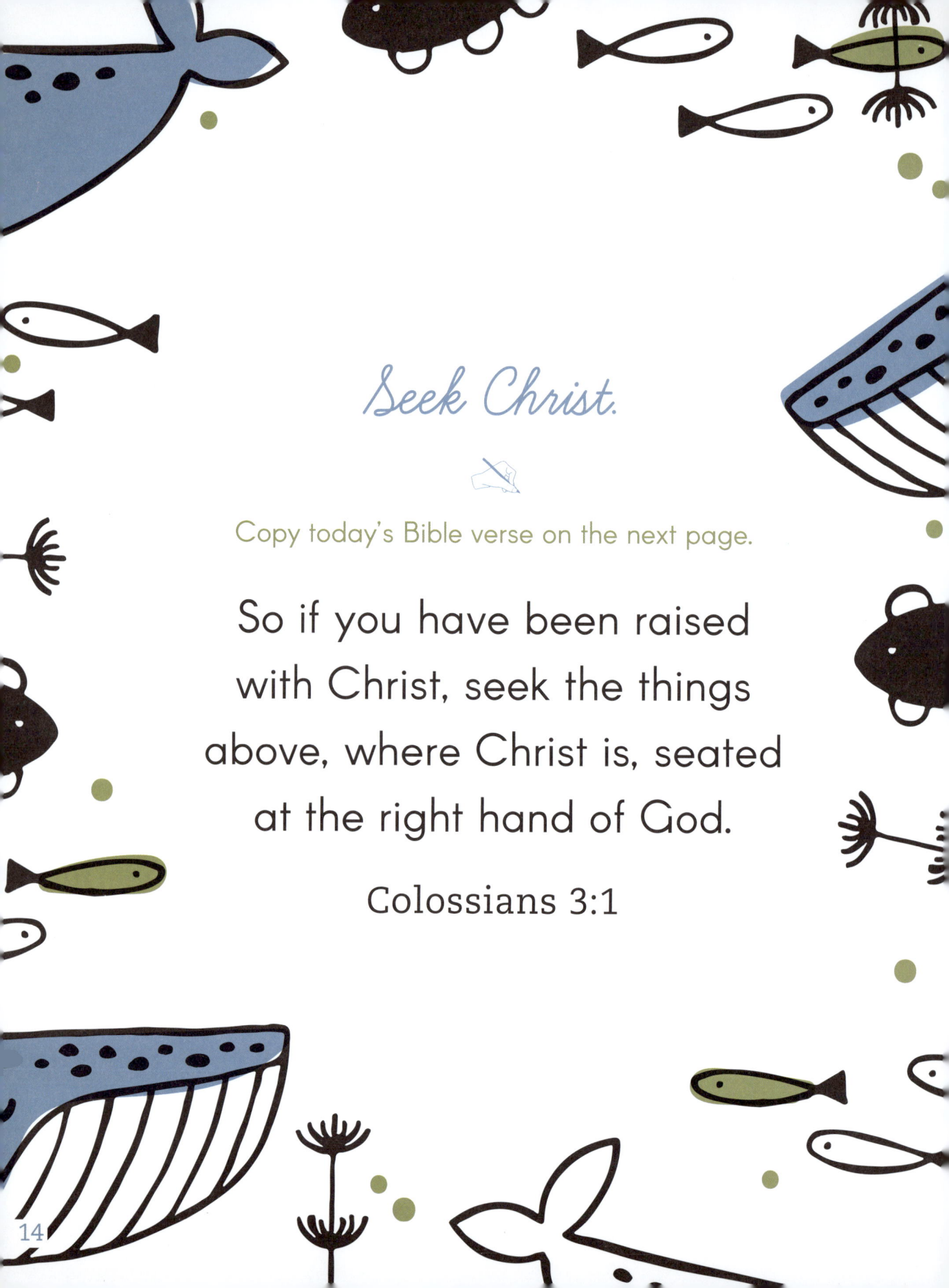

Copy today's Bible verse on the next page.

So if you have been raised with Christ, seek the things above, where Christ is, seated at the right hand of God.

Colossians 3:1

First, write your name.

Then, write the verse.

You are free.

Copy today's Bible verse on the next page.

So if the Son sets you free, you really will be free.

John 8:36

First, write your name.

Then, write the verse.

Shine light into darkness.

Copy today's Bible verse on the next page.

Don't participate in the fruitless works of darkness, but instead expose them.

Ephesians 5:11

First, write your name.

Then, write the verse.

Glorify God.

Copy today's Bible verse on the next page.

You are not your own, for you were bought at a price. So glorify God with your body.

1 Corinthians 6:20

First, write your name.

Then, write the verse.

You are under grace.

Copy today's Bible verse on the next page.

For sin will not rule over you, because you are not under the law but under grace.

Romans 6:14

First, write your name.

Then, write the verse.

Live with Christ.

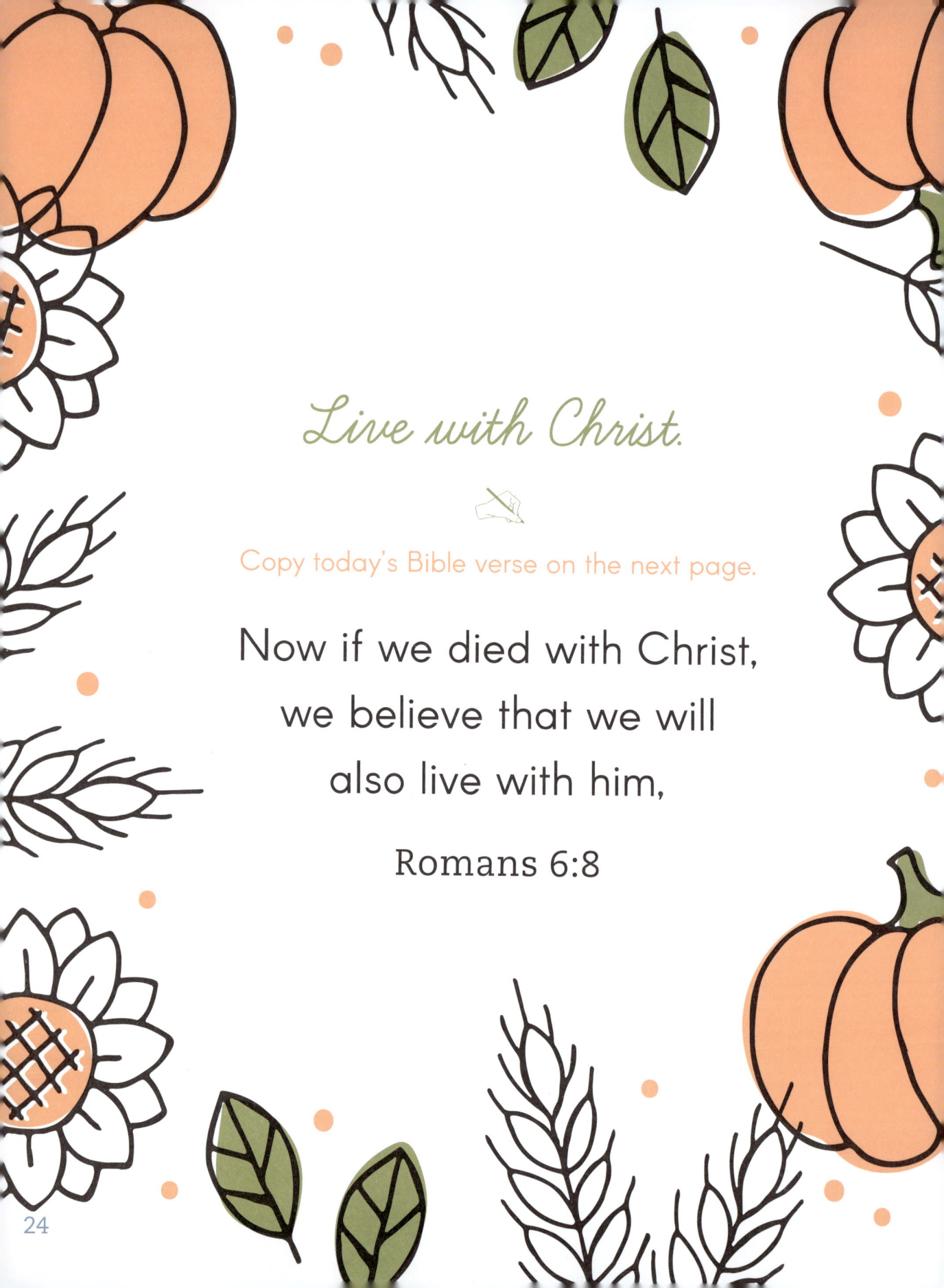

Copy today's Bible verse on the next page.

Now if we died with Christ, we believe that we will also live with him,

Romans 6:8

First, write your name.

Then, write the verse.

Don't live in sin.

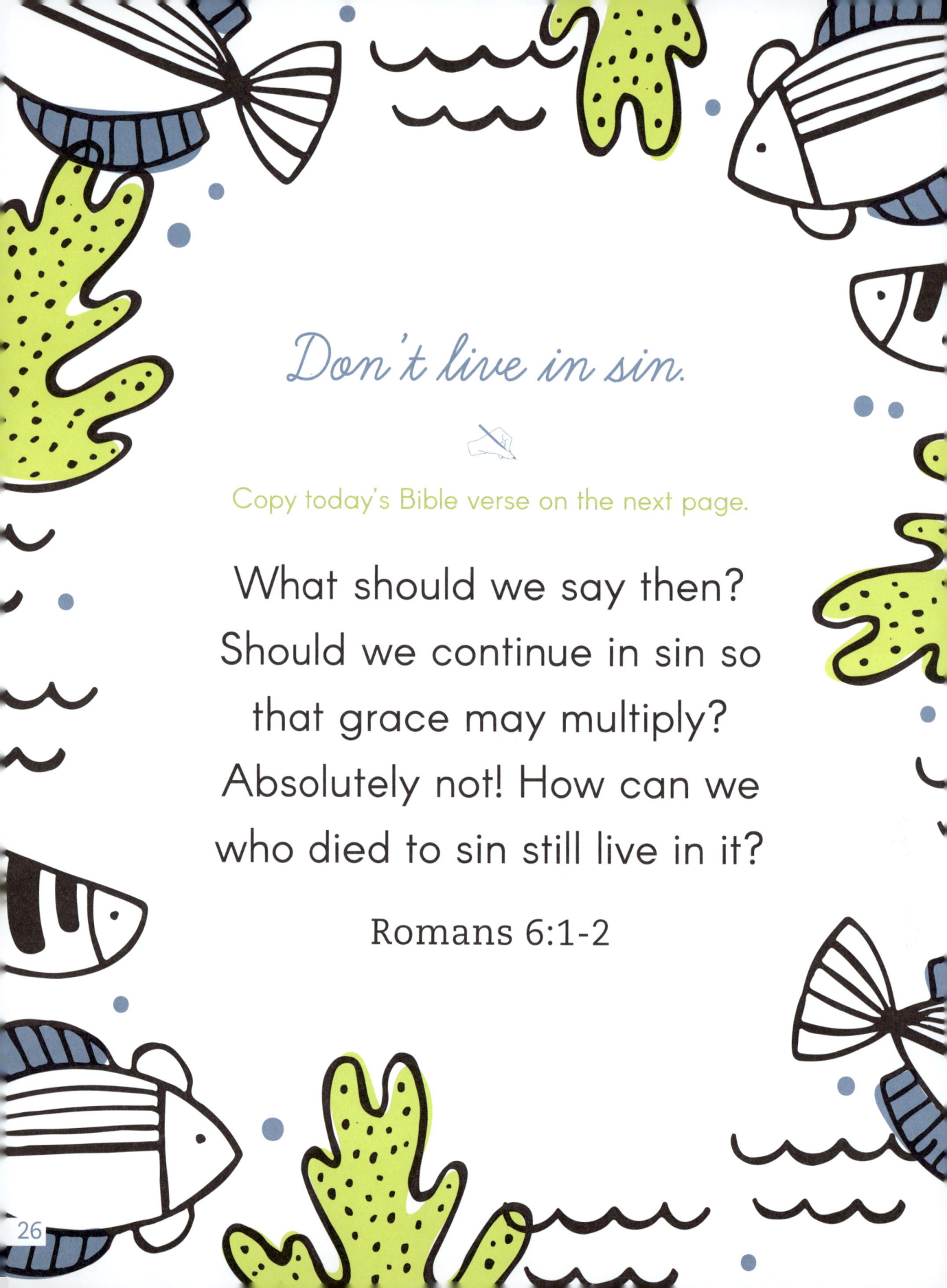

Copy today's Bible verse on the next page.

What should we say then? Should we continue in sin so that grace may multiply? Absolutely not! How can we who died to sin still live in it?

Romans 6:1-2

First, write your name.

Then, write the verse.

Confess your sins.

Copy today's Bible verse on the next page.

If we confess our sins, he is faithful and righteous to forgive us our sins and to cleanse us from all unrighteousness.

1 John 1:9

First, write your name.

Then, write the verse.

Renew your mind.

Copy today's Bible verse on the next page.

Do not be conformed to this age, but be transformed by the renewing of your mind, so that you may discern what is the good, pleasing, and perfect will of God.

Romans 12:2

First, write your name.

Then, write the verse.

You are a child of God.

Copy today's Bible verse on the next page.

But to all who did receive him, he gave them the right to be children of God, to those who believe in his name,

John 1:12

First, write your name.

Then, write the verse.

Be joined to the Lord.

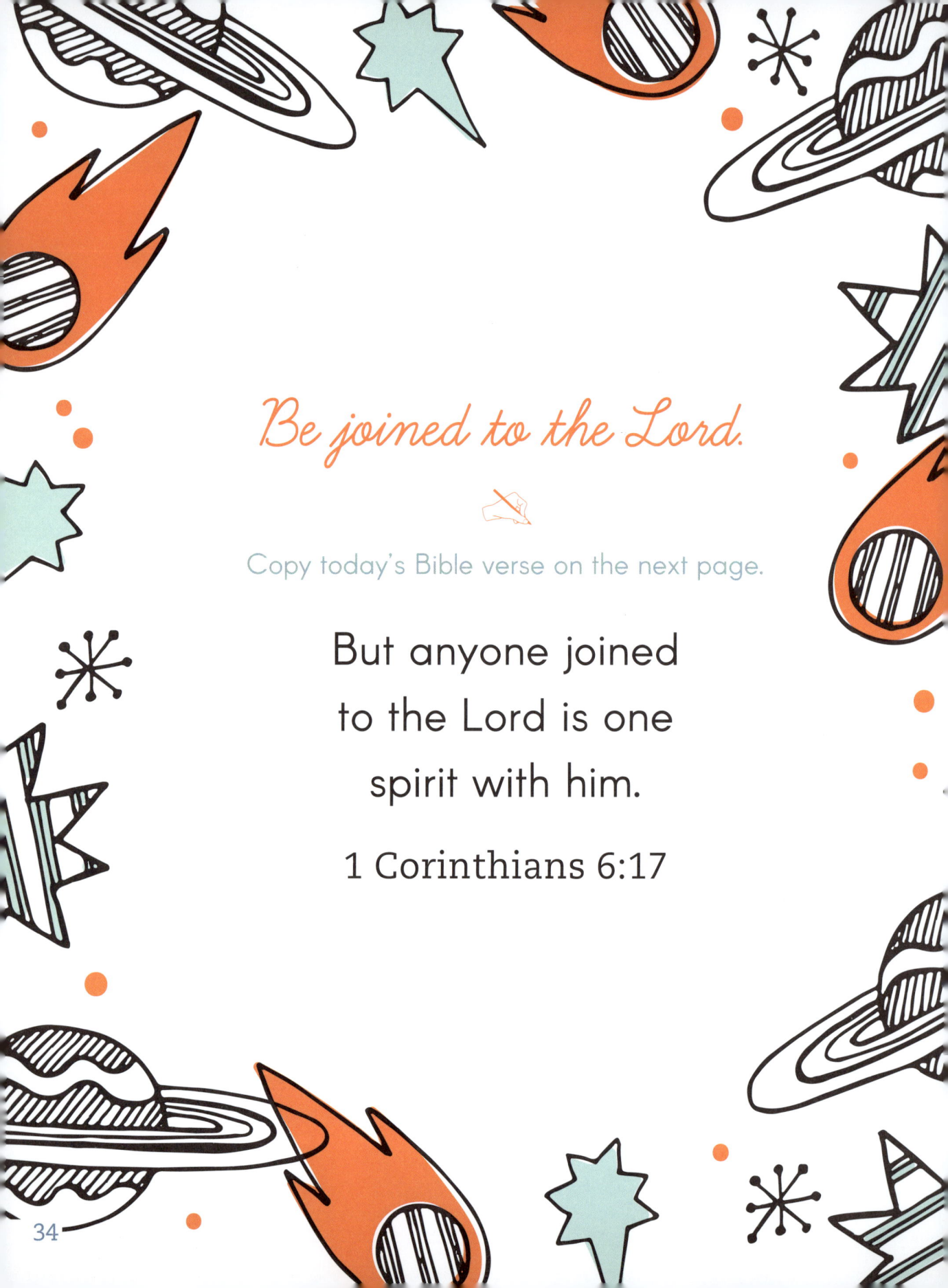

Copy today's Bible verse on the next page.

But anyone joined to the Lord is one spirit with him.

1 Corinthians 6:17

First, write your name.

Then, write the verse.

You are freed from sin.

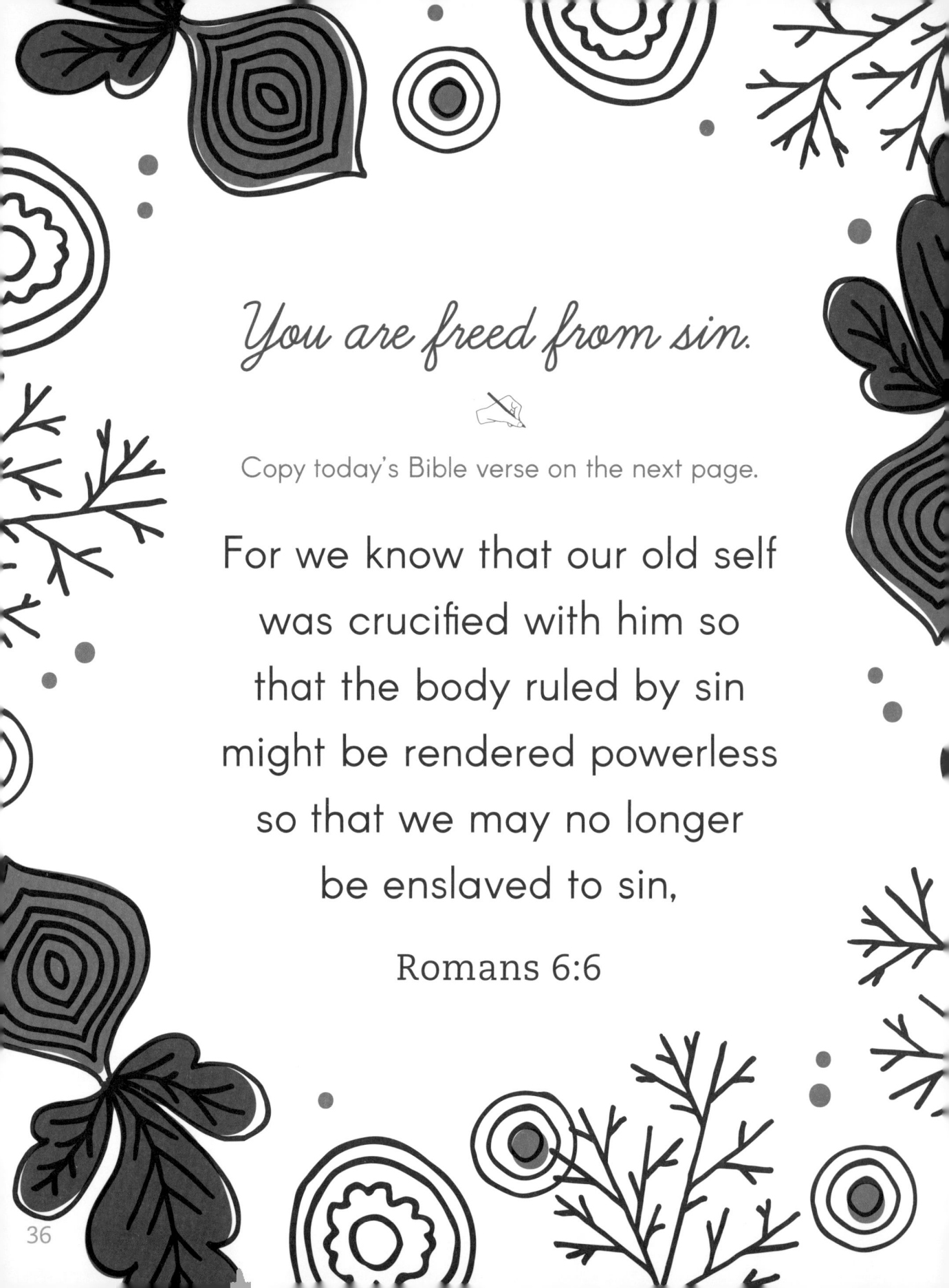

Copy today's Bible verse on the next page.

For we know that our old self was crucified with him so that the body ruled by sin might be rendered powerless so that we may no longer be enslaved to sin,

Romans 6:6

First, write your name.

Then, write the verse.

You are the body of Christ.

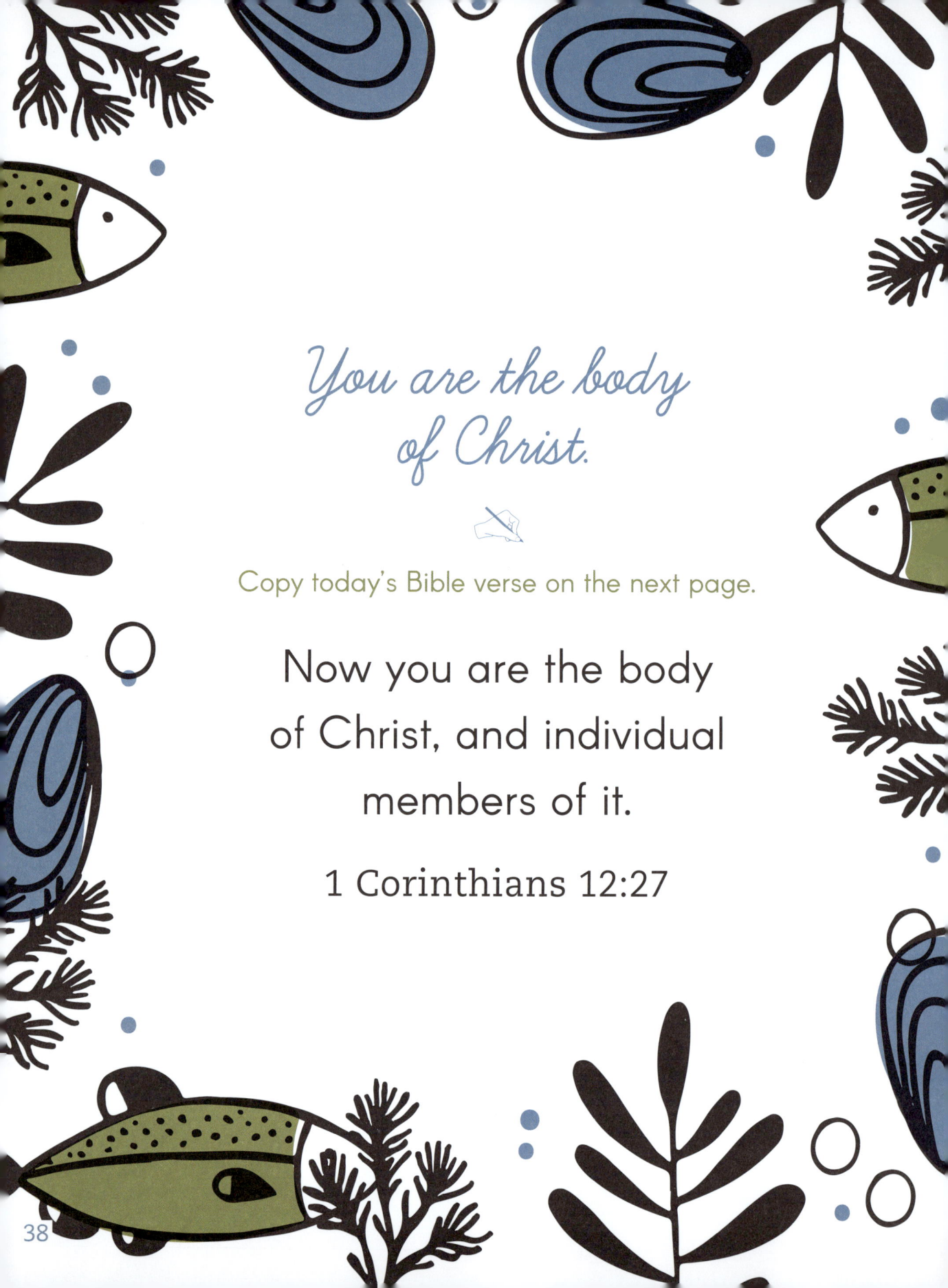

Copy today's Bible verse on the next page.

Now you are the body of Christ, and individual members of it.

1 Corinthians 12:27

First, write your name.

Then, write the verse.

Proclaim His praises.

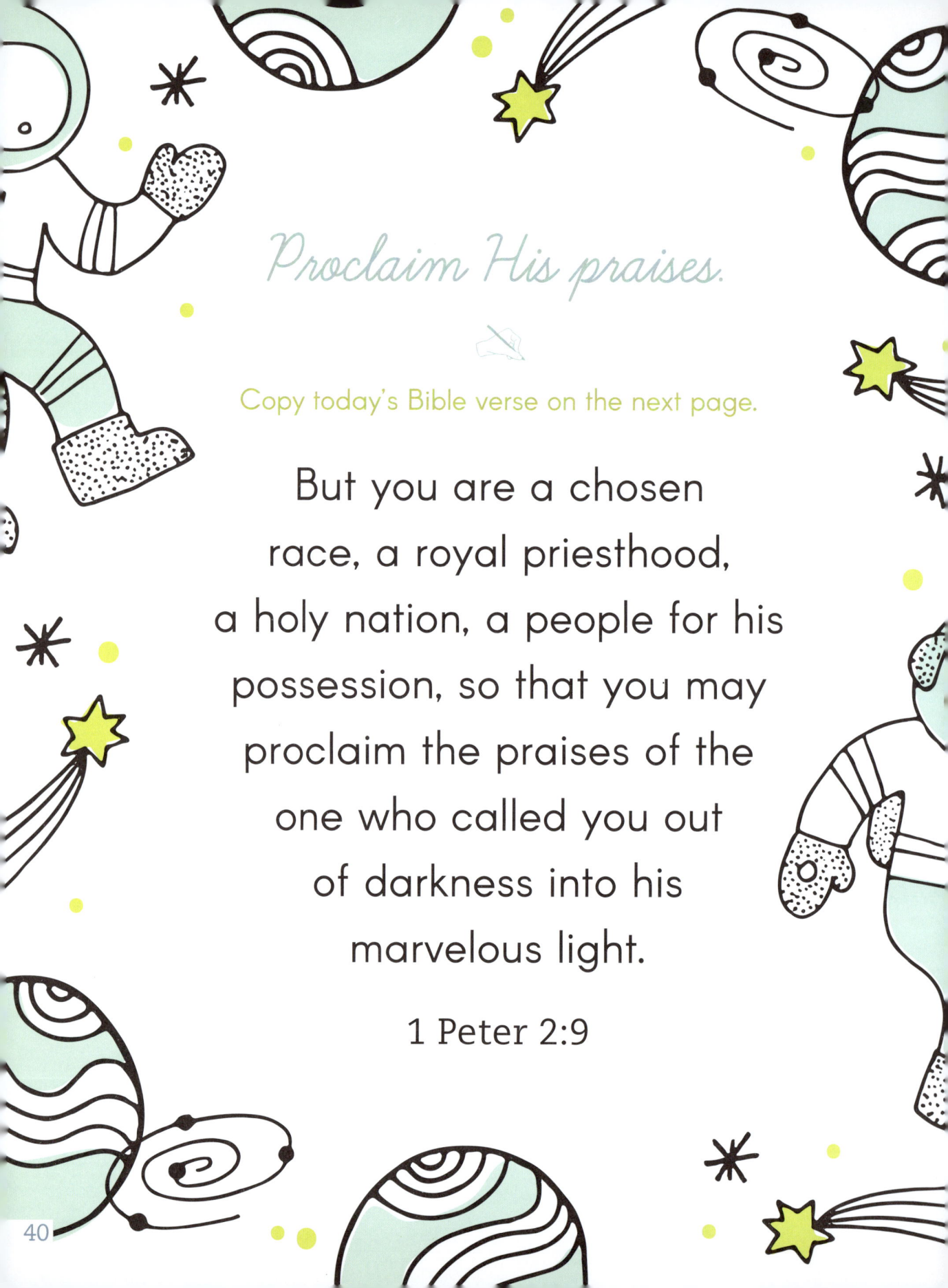

Copy today's Bible verse on the next page.

But you are a chosen race, a royal priesthood, a holy nation, a people for his possession, so that you may proclaim the praises of the one who called you out of darkness into his marvelous light.

1 Peter 2:9

First, write your name.

Then, write the verse.

We are more than conquerors.

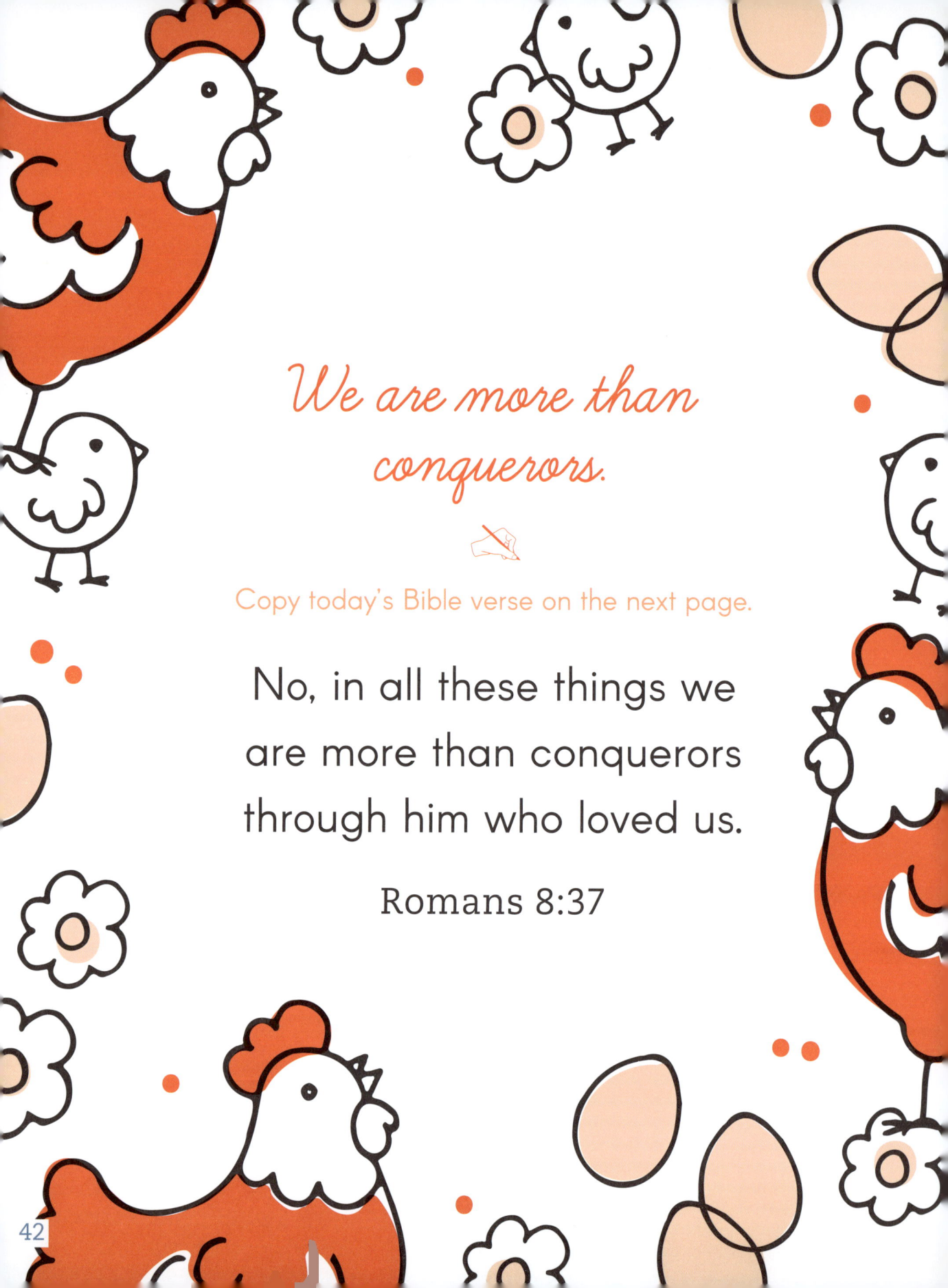

Copy today's Bible verse on the next page.

No, in all these things we are more than conquerors through him who loved us.

Romans 8:37

First, write your name.

Then, write the verse.

Remain in Christ.

Copy today's Bible verse on the next page.

Remain in me, and I in you. Just as a branch is unable to produce fruit by itself unless it remains on the vine, neither can you unless you remain in me.

John 15:4

First, write your name.

Then, write the verse.

Keep His commands.

Copy today's Bible verse on the next page.

If you keep my commands you will remain in my love, just as I have kept my Father's commands and remain in his love.

John 15:10

First, write your name.

Then, write the verse.

Go and produce fruit.

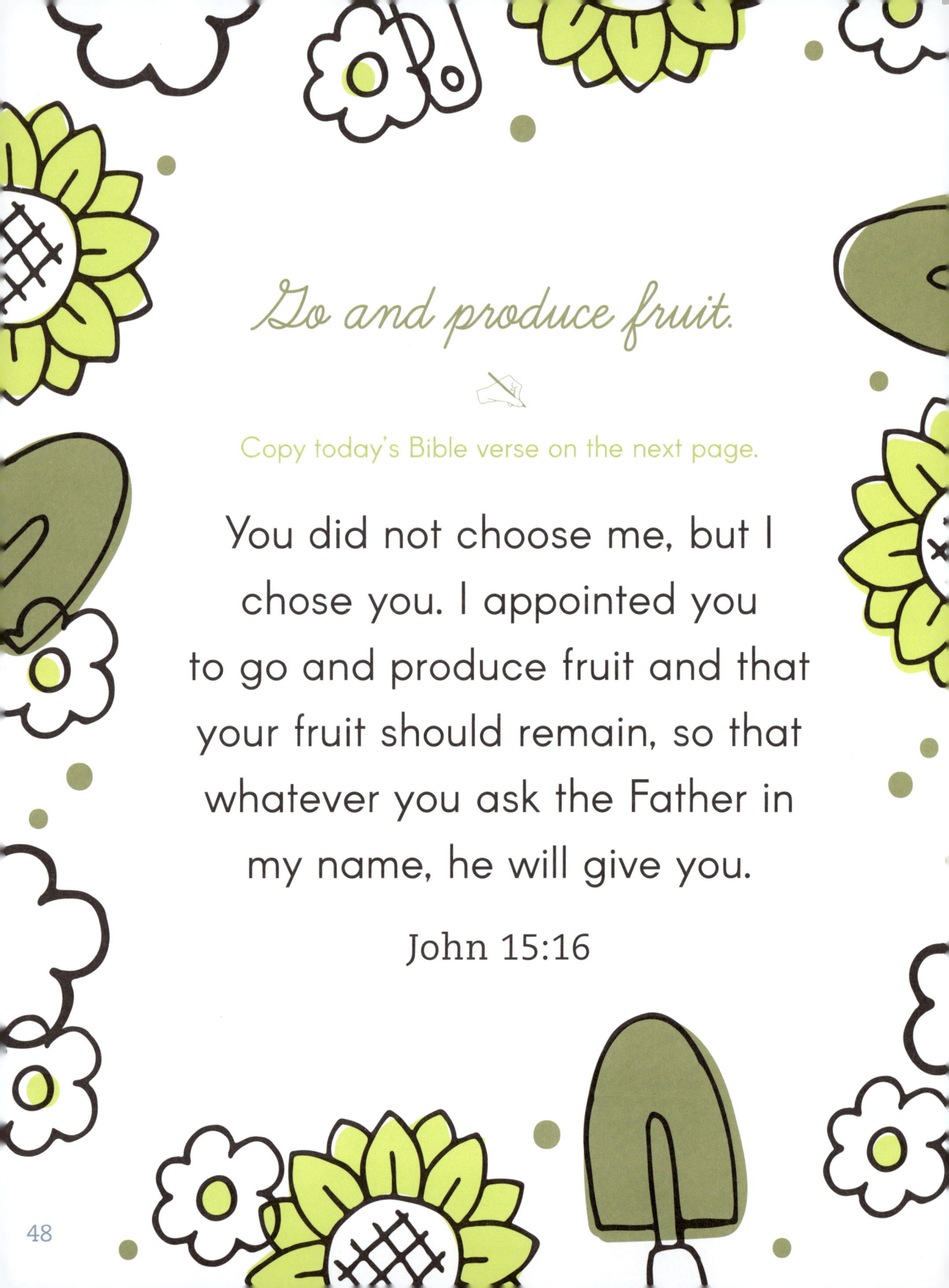

Copy today's Bible verse on the next page.

You did not choose me, but I chose you. I appointed you to go and produce fruit and that your fruit should remain, so that whatever you ask the Father in my name, he will give you.

John 15:16

First, write your name.

Then, write the verse.

Put on the new self.

Copy today's Bible verse on the next page.

Do not lie to one another, since you have put off the old self with its practices and have put on the new self. You are being renewed in knowledge according to the image of your Creator.

Colossians 3:9-10

First, write your name.

Then, write the verse.

Forgive as He forgave.

Copy today's Bible verse on the next page.

Just as the Lord has forgiven you, so you are also to forgive.

Colossians 3:13

First, write your name.

Then, write the verse.

Be thankful.

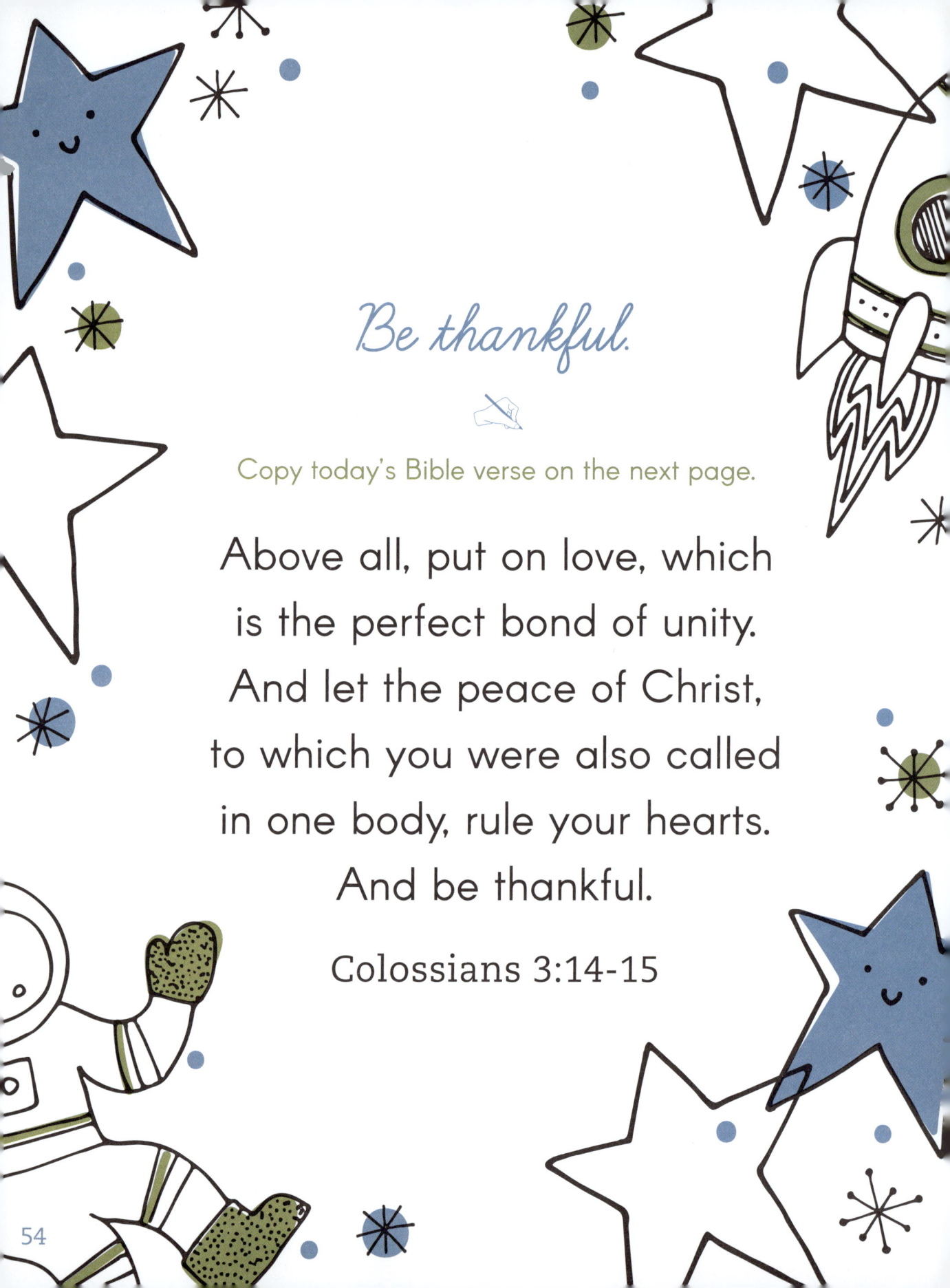

Copy today's Bible verse on the next page.

Above all, put on love, which is the perfect bond of unity. And let the peace of Christ, to which you were also called in one body, rule your hearts. And be thankful.

Colossians 3:14-15

First, write your name.

Then, write the verse.

Sing to God with gratitude.

Copy today's Bible verse on the next page.

Let the word of Christ dwell richly among you, in all wisdom teaching and admonishing one another through psalms, hymns, and spiritual songs, singing to God with gratitude in your hearts.

Colossians 3:16

First, write your name.

Then, write the verse.

Do everything in the name of the Lord.

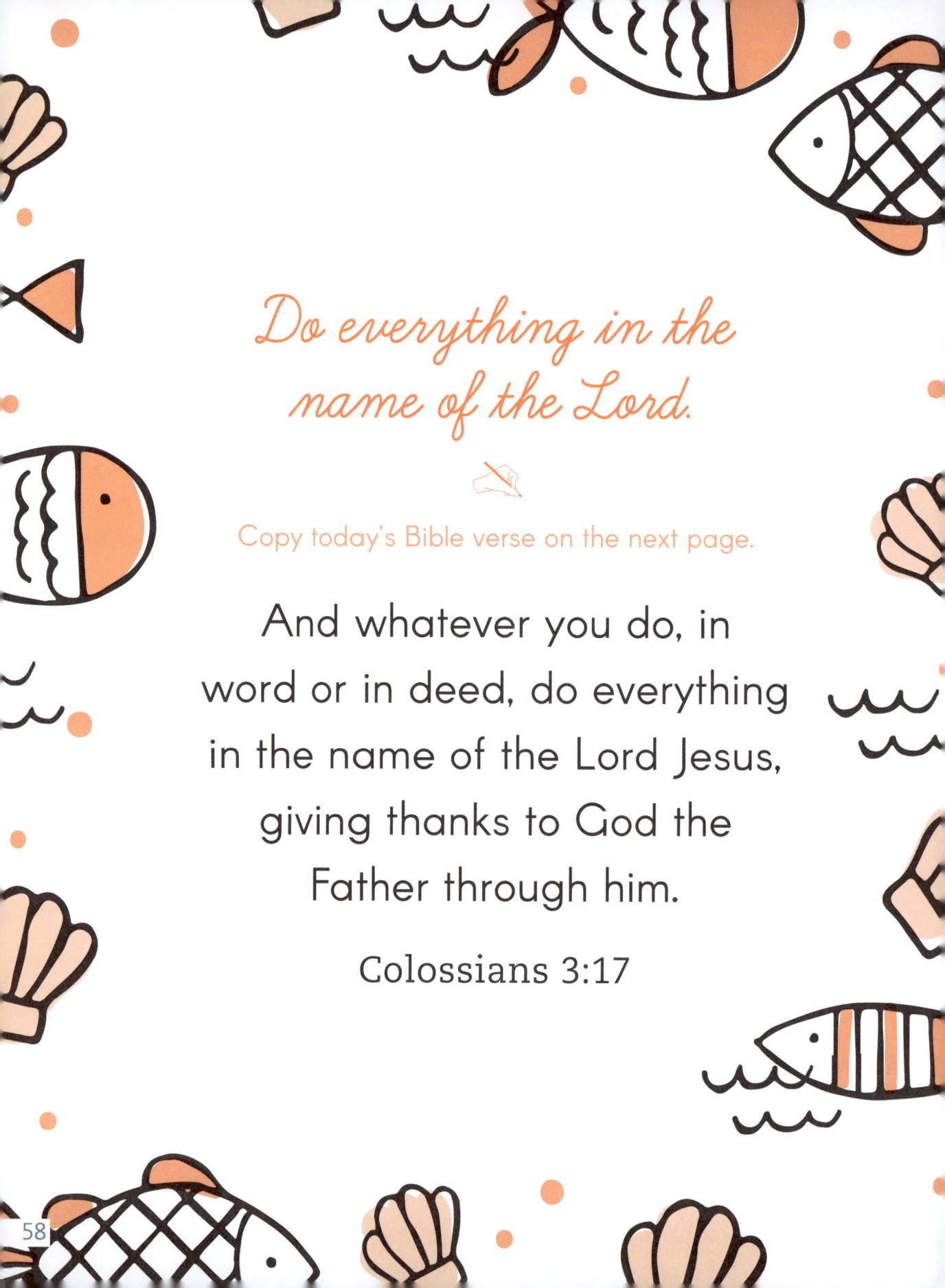

Copy today's Bible verse on the next page.

And whatever you do, in word or in deed, do everything in the name of the Lord Jesus, giving thanks to God the Father through him.

Colossians 3:17

First, write your name.

Then, write the verse.

Obey your parents.

Copy today's Bible verse on the next page.

Children, obey your parents in everything, for this pleases the Lord.

Colossians 3:20

First, write your name.

Then, write the verse.

Do all things for the Lord.

Copy today's Bible verse on the next page.

Whatever you do, do it from the heart, as something done for the Lord and not for people,

Colossians 3:23

First, write your name.

Then, write the verse.

You were made for heaven.

Copy today's Bible verse on the next page.

Our citizenship is in heaven, and we eagerly wait for a Savior from there, the Lord Jesus Christ.

Philippians 3:20

First, write your name.

Then, write the verse.

Be rooted in Christ.

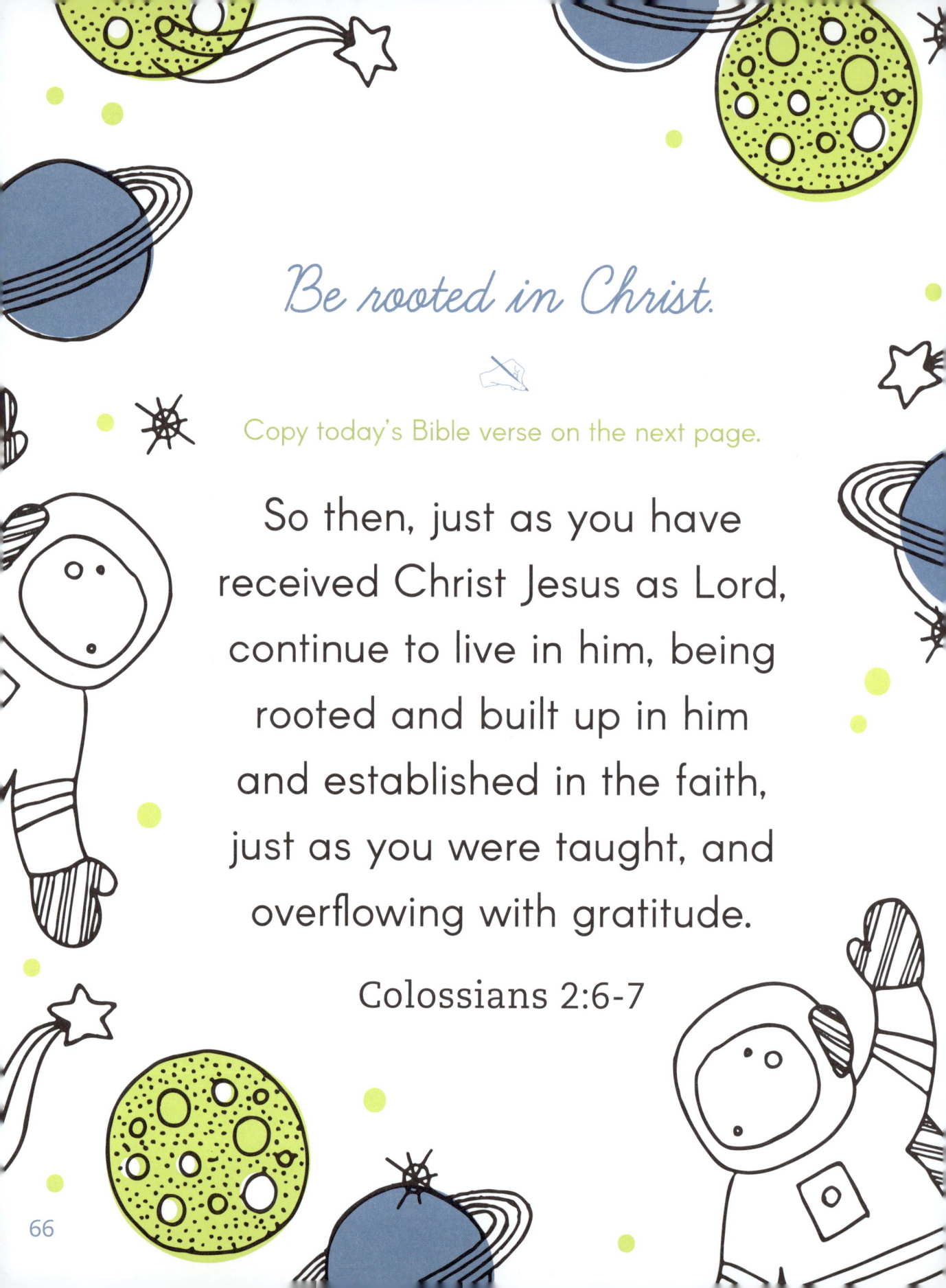

Copy today's Bible verse on the next page.

So then, just as you have received Christ Jesus as Lord, continue to live in him, being rooted and built up in him and established in the faith, just as you were taught, and overflowing with gratitude.

Colossians 2:6-7

First, write your name.

Then, write the verse.

Be reconciled to God.

Copy today's Bible verse on the next page.

Therefore, we are ambassadors for Christ, since God is making his appeal through us. We plead on Christ's behalf: "Be reconciled to God."

2 Corinthians 5:20

First, write your name.

Then, write the verse.

Trust God for your needs.

Copy today's Bible verse on the next page.

And my God will supply all your needs according to his riches in glory in Christ Jesus.

Philippians 4:19

First, write your name.

Then, write the verse.

You are a light.

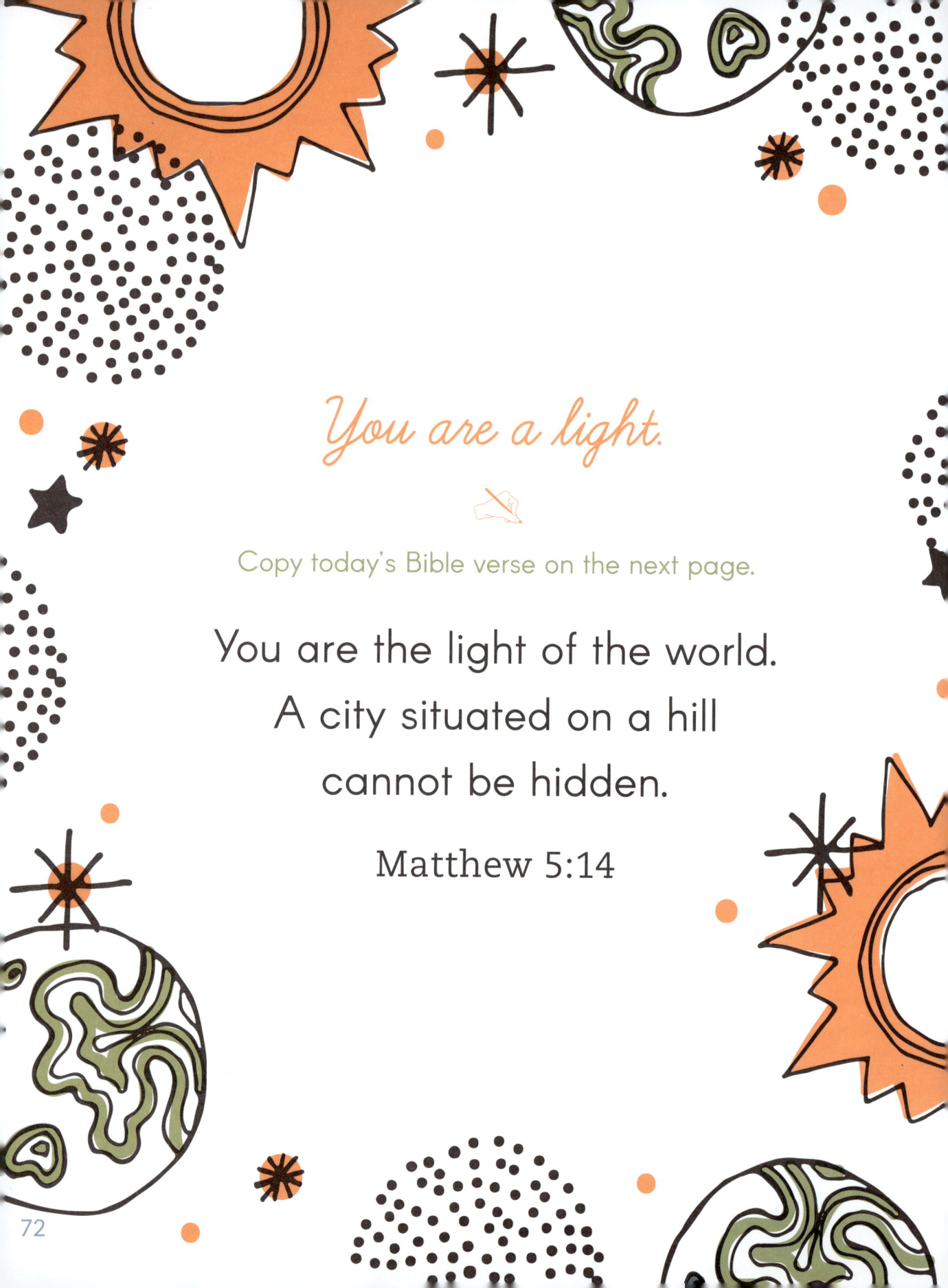

Copy today's Bible verse on the next page.

You are the light of the world. A city situated on a hill cannot be hidden.

Matthew 5:14

First, write your name.

Then, write the verse.

Be children of light.

Copy today's Bible verse on the next page.

For you were once darkness, but now you are light in the Lord. Live as children of light—

Ephesians 5:8

First, write your name.

Then, write the verse.

You are declared righteous.

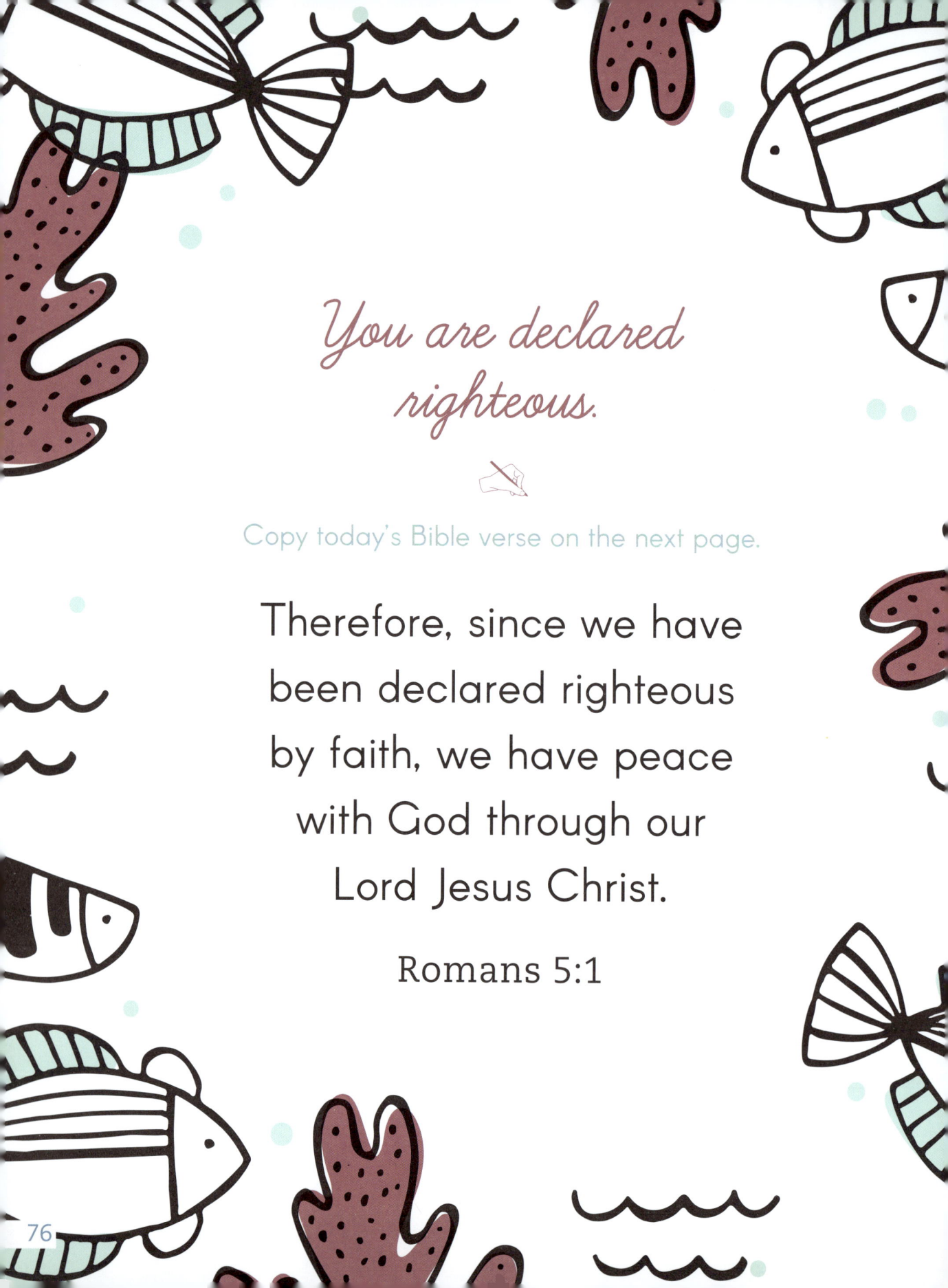

Copy today's Bible verse on the next page.

Therefore, since we have been declared righteous by faith, we have peace with God through our Lord Jesus Christ.

Romans 5:1

First, write
your name.

Then, write
the verse.

You are saved by grace!

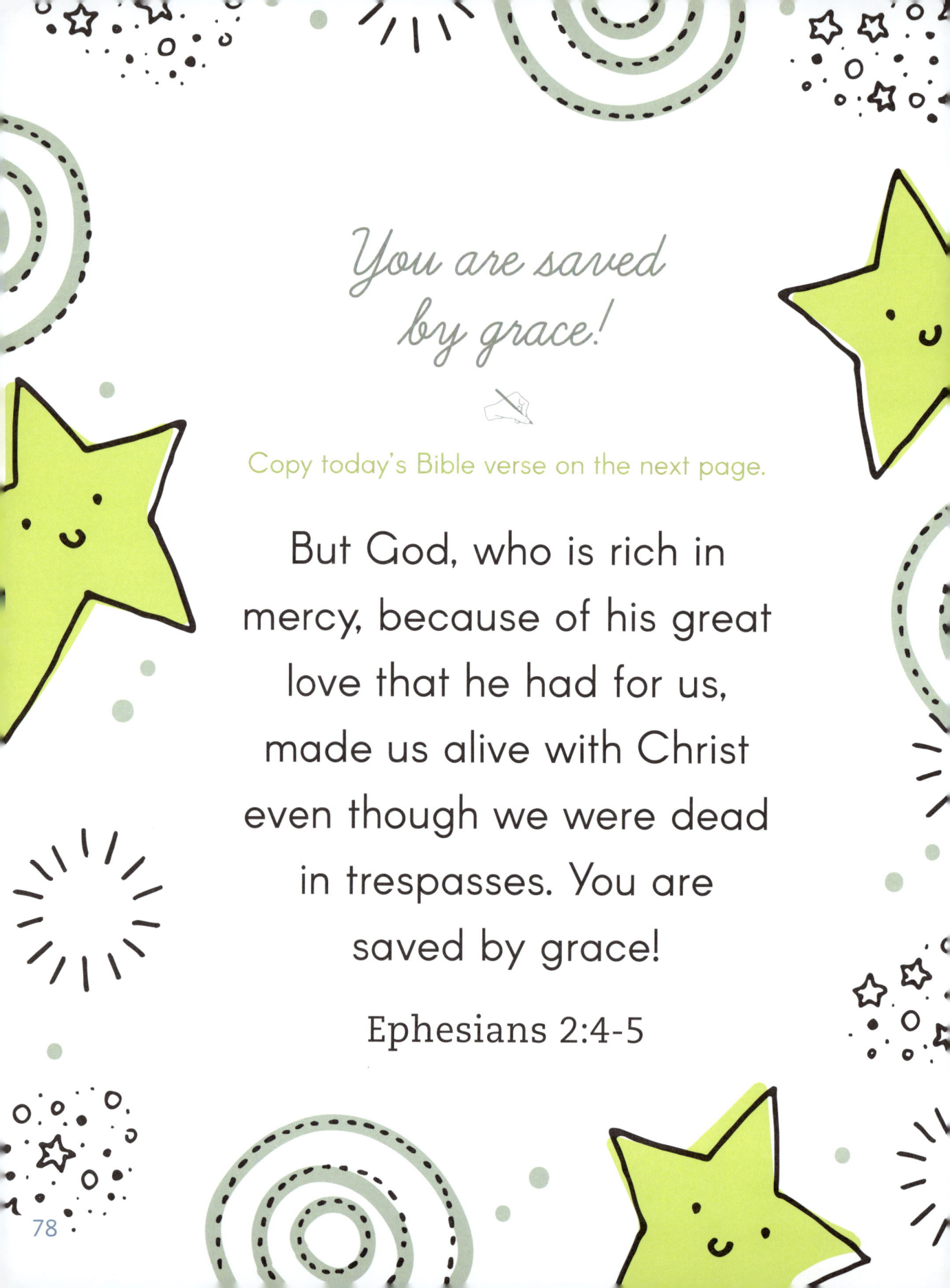

Copy today's Bible verse on the next page.

But God, who is rich in mercy, because of his great love that he had for us, made us alive with Christ even though we were dead in trespasses. You are saved by grace!

Ephesians 2:4-5

First, write your name.

Then, write the verse.

God is with you.

Copy today's Bible verse on the next page.

God, how precious your thoughts are to me; how vast their sum is! If I counted them, they would outnumber the grains of sand; when I wake up, I am still with you.

Psalm 139:17-18

First, write your name.

Then, write the verse.

Walk by the Spirit.

Copy today's Bible verse on the next page.

I say then, walk by the Spirit and you will certainly not carry out the desire of the flesh.

Galatians 5:16

First, write your name.

Then, write the verse.

Joy is your hope.

Copy today's Bible verse on the next page.

The hope of the righteous is joy, but the expectation of the wicked will perish.

Proverbs 10:28

First, write your name.

Then, write the verse.

Rejoice with joy.

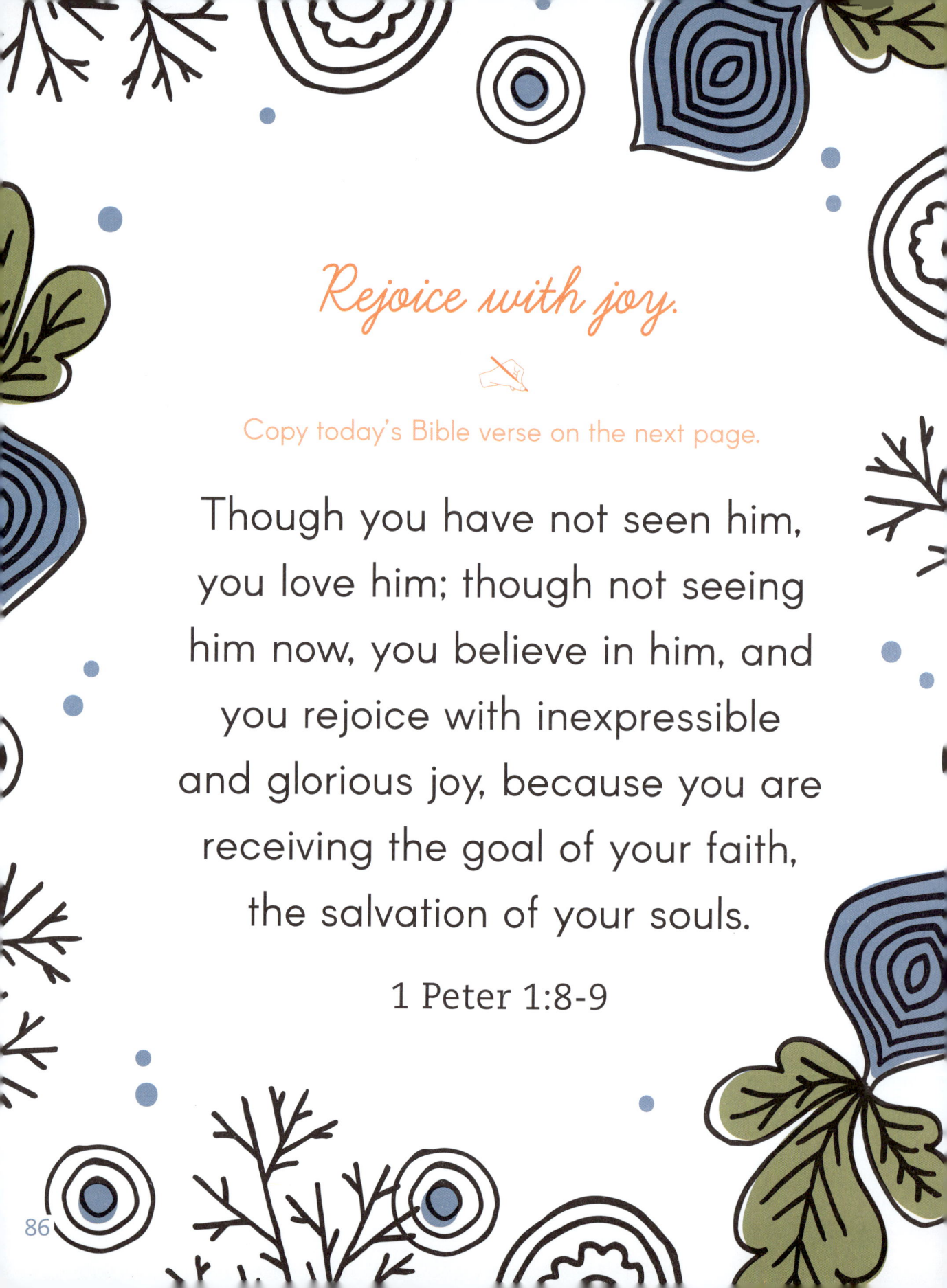

Copy today's Bible verse on the next page.

Though you have not seen him, you love him; though not seeing him now, you believe in him, and you rejoice with inexpressible and glorious joy, because you are receiving the goal of your faith, the salvation of your souls.

1 Peter 1:8-9

First, write your name.

Then, write the verse.

Overflow with hope.

Copy today's Bible verse on the next page.

Now may the God of hope fill you with all joy and peace as you believe so that you may overflow with hope by the power of the Holy Spirit.

Romans 15:13

First, write your name.

Then, write the verse.

Be content.

Copy today's Bible verse on the next page.

I know how to make do with little, and I know how to make do with a lot. In any and all circumstances I have learned the secret of being content—whether well fed or hungry, whether in abundance or in need.

Philippians 4:12

First, write your name.

Then, write the verse.

Live for Christ.

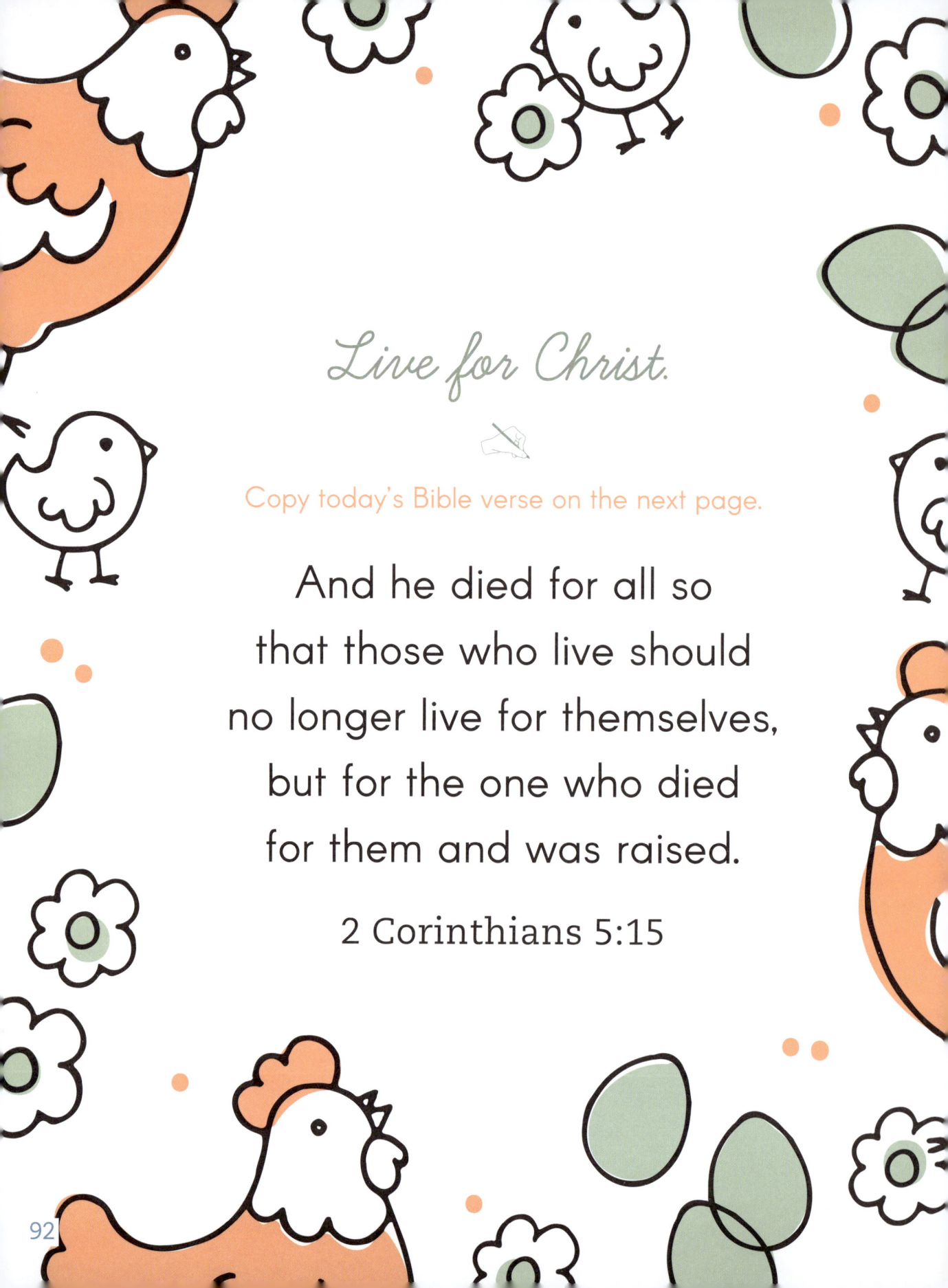

Copy today's Bible verse on the next page.

And he died for all so that those who live should no longer live for themselves, but for the one who died for them and was raised.

2 Corinthians 5:15

First, write your name.

Then, write the verse.

Walk in the light.

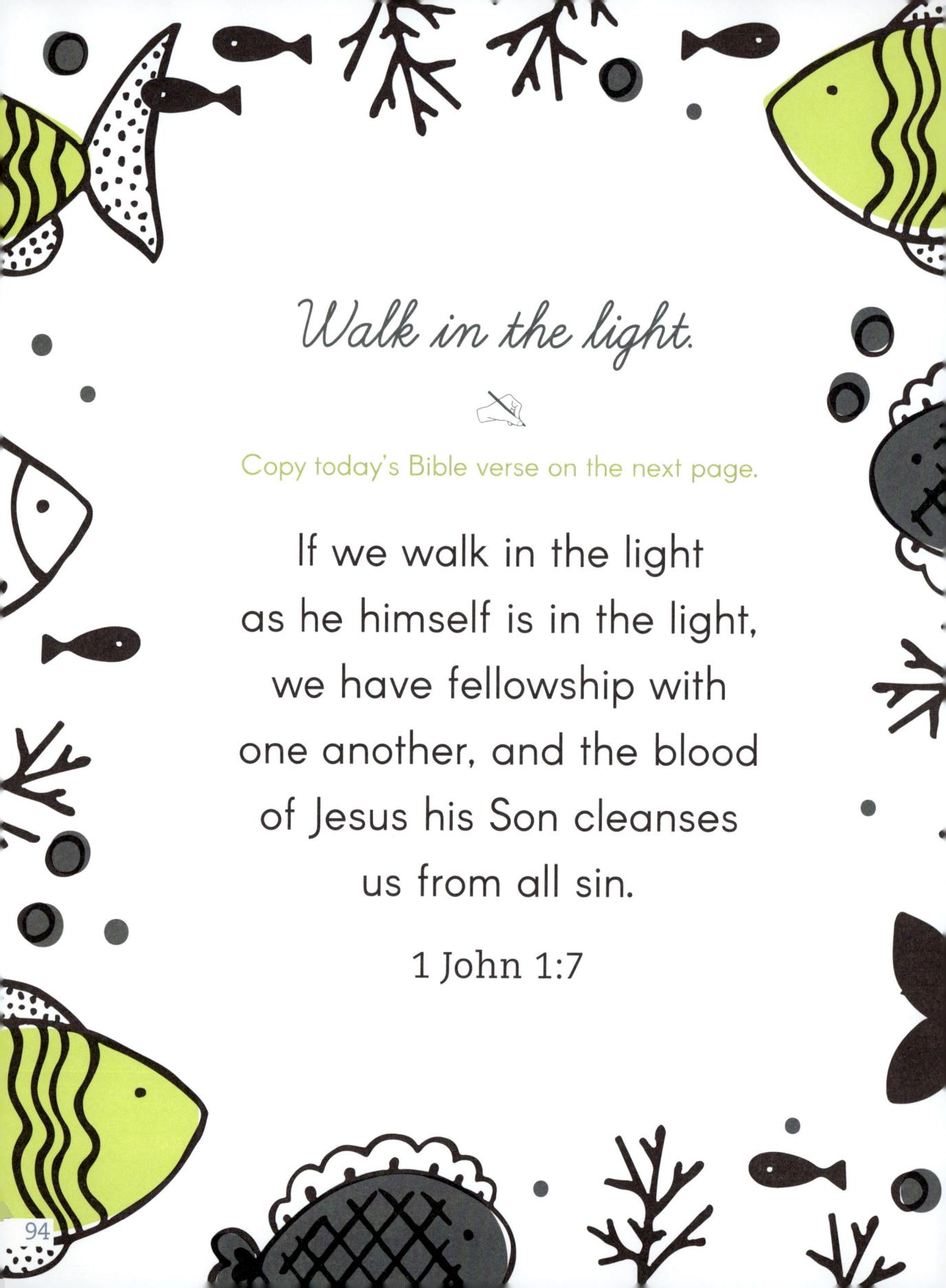

Copy today's Bible verse on the next page.

If we walk in the light as he himself is in the light, we have fellowship with one another, and the blood of Jesus his Son cleanses us from all sin.

1 John 1:7

First, write your name.

Then, write the verse.

Love one another.

Copy today's Bible verse on the next page.

For the whole law is fulfilled in one statement: Love your neighbor as yourself.

Galatians 5:14

First, write your name.

Then, write the verse.

Live by the Spirit.

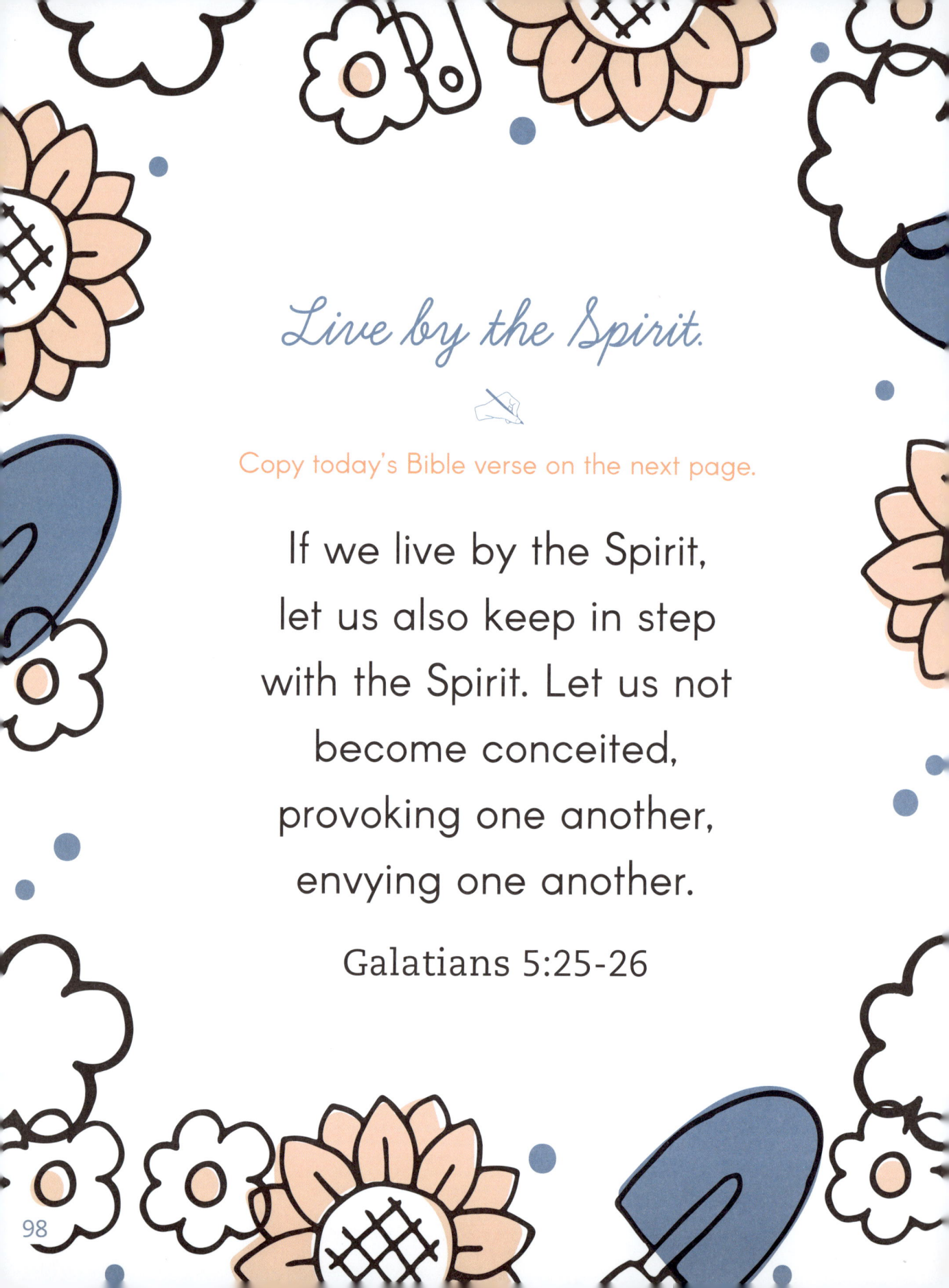

Copy today's Bible verse on the next page.

If we live by the Spirit, let us also keep in step with the Spirit. Let us not become conceited, provoking one another, envying one another.

Galatians 5:25-26

First, write your name.

Then, write the verse.

Be steadfast.

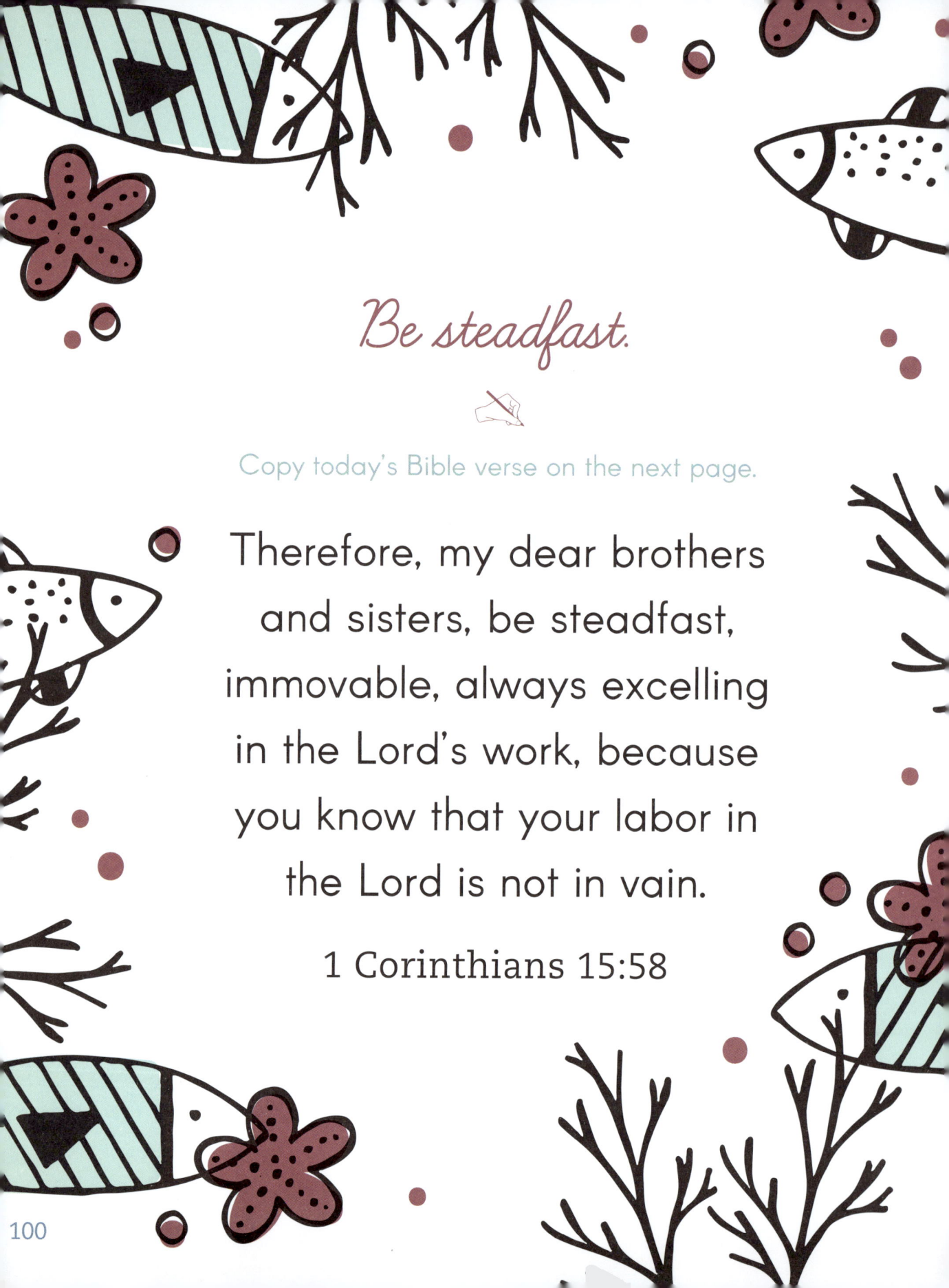

Copy today's Bible verse on the next page.

Therefore, my dear brothers and sisters, be steadfast, immovable, always excelling in the Lord's work, because you know that your labor in the Lord is not in vain.

1 Corinthians 15:58

First, write your name.

Then, write the verse.

Keep His commands.

Copy today's Bible verse on the next page.

If you love me, you will keep my commands. And I will ask the Father, and he will give you another Counselor to be with you forever.

John 14:15-16

First, write your name.

Then, write the verse.

Thank You

for studying God's Word with us!

CONNECT WITH US

@thedailygraceco
@kristinschmucker

CONTACT US

info@thedailygraceco.com

SHARE

#thedailygraceco
#lampandlight

WEBSITE

www.thedailygraceco.com